Detours

10 Roadblocks to the Great Commission

Paul Seger

CONTENTS

PREFACE

Most churches have never sent a missionary from their congregation. This is ironic since these same churches love missions and missionaries. They have a missions budget and support missionaries. They have a missions committee. They are likely to have a missions conference or missions emphasis weekends. They pray for missionaries. They decorate the walls of their buildings with pictures of missionaries they support. Yet despite all this, they may never have launched an international worker from their pews, or it may have been 30 years since they did that.

BMW (Biblical Ministries Worldwide) wanted to know why this inconsistency exists, so we recently conducted five THINK TANKS with groups of pastors in four different states. The discussion topic was how churches could identify, train and launch missionaries from their congregation. One of the questions we asked was: Why would a church NOT want to send missionaries from their congregation? This book is a summary of those pastors' answers to this question.

Be assured that this book is not intended to be critical of pastors. They have one of the most difficult jobs in the world. In their leadership role they have to accomplish everything any corporate leader is called to do, PLUS they have to do it with volunteers who, in many cases, contribute to their salary. It is with utmost respect and appreciation for pastors that we addressed this topic. The chapter headings of this book are not mine . . . they were given to us by pastors as they critiqued themselves.

If your church has not recently sent a missionary from your congregation, this book may help you discover why that is true and offer ways to overcome some of the roadblocks that are creating detours.

INTRODUCTION: DETOURS

I hate detours. They slow down forward progress. They add miles and minutes to the journey. They are frustrating. They result in a slower speed limit and probably more traffic. They mean a late arrival. A detour is signaled by a roadblock, a temporary barricade that forces traffic off the main road to a side road, and I hate barricades. A roadblock is a euphemism for something that prevents accomplishment of a goal. What is to like about that?

Roadblocks are, however, put in the way for a reason. There may be an accident ahead, or the road may be washed out, necessitating a detour. This book will examine the reasons for roadblocks to sending missionaries from your church. There may be some accident or road washed out in the life of your church that is hindering forward progress with the Great Commission. Ultimately, leaders must take responsibility for fixing the road ahead and, in some instances, the leader needs fixing since the pastor could be the reason for the detour.

It could be possible for churches to be on a detour doing many good things and not be on the main road of the Great Commission. Even though they have taken a side road, they are still moving forward but not at the speed and efficiency of traveling on the main highway. This book is an attempt to address some of the reasons why churches are on detours . . . particularly where it relates to the Great Commission.

Their path may eventually get them to a destination, but eliminating the detour could get them there a lot faster. This book is about staying on the main road.

Following are ten reasons pastors in these think tanks gave us as to why churches may not be sending missionaries.

REASON #1: CONGREGATIONAL EXPECTATIONS

Serving as a pastor is an incredibly challenging task. It is like having multiple bosses. Everyone in the church has a different idea about what the pastor should be doing and what his job description should look like. Church members will vote with their feet if the pastor is not meeting their expectations. They have some generic expectations of the pastor: preach good sermons, be available to visit us in the hospital, counsel, and perform weddings and funerals. These expectations leave little time for pastors to focus on training future leaders. Thus, the first reason churches and pastors are not identifying, training and sending out tomorrow's missionaries is that congregants may have expectations that don't allow pastors to focus their time on equipping a few leaders.

In addition to that, each church member nuances his own personal job description for his pastor. Jesus said, "*You leave the commandment of God and hold to the tradition of men. And he said to them, 'You have a fine way of rejecting the commandment of God in order to establish your own tradition'*" (Mark 7:8-9). In this passage, the Jews were doing a good thing, relinquishing their possessions to the temple, but they weren't caring for their parents. They left the biblical for the cultural. Could it be possible that there are church members who have come up with their own *traditions of men* that put unrealistic expectations on the job description of their pastor?

In view of this, it is critical for a pastor to make scripture his "boss" and chiefly be concerned about pleasing Jesus, the head of the church. According to Scripture, here is the job description of a pastor:

1. TRAIN: *And he gave the apostles, the prophets, the evangelists, the shepherds and teachers, to equip the saints for the work of ministry, for building up the body of Christ* (Ephesians 4:11-12).

   And what you have heard from me in the presence of many witnesses entrust to faithful men, who will be able to teach others also (2 Timothy 2:2).

2. CARE: *Shepherd the flock of God that is among you, exercising oversight* (1 Peter 5:2-3).

   For they are keeping watch over your souls, as those who will have to give an account (Hebrews 13:17).

3. MODEL: *Therefore an overseer must be above reproach* (1 Timothy 3:2).

   Not domineering over those in your charge, but being examples to the flock (1 Peter 5:3).

4. PRAY: *Is anyone among you sick? Let him call for the elders of the church, and let them pray over him, anointing him with oil in the name of the Lord* (James 5:14).

   But we will devote ourselves to prayer and to the ministry of the word (Acts 6:4).

5. TEACH: *Let the elders who rule well be considered worthy of double honor, especially those who labor in preaching and teaching* (1 Timothy 5:17).

6. GUARD: *Therefore I testify to you this day that I am innocent of the blood of all, for I did not shrink from declaring to you the whole counsel of God. Pay careful attention to yourselves and to all the flock, in which the Holy Spirit has made you overseers, to care for the church of God, which he obtained with his own blood. I know that after my departure fierce wolves will come in among you, not sparing the flock; and from among your own selves will arise men speaking twisted things, to draw away the disciples after them. Therefore be alert, remembering that for three years I did not cease night or day to admonish every one with tears* (Acts 20:26-31).

While individual churches may wish to add more to a pastor's job description, this is what the head of the church said about the topic. It would seem appropriate to ask a pastor to focus on these things first and then, if there is time left over, to do the other things church members expect. It would seem prudent for the pastor to be secure and satisfied with the job description that God gives and not cave in to the other expectations of church members. It is not possible to please everyone, so why not just try to please the Lord?

LEADERS TRAIN LEADERS

The first item in this job description is the role of training others to do ministry. We have traditionally outsourced this to colleges and seminaries. Our expectation is that institutions will handle training for us. They are the specialists and are an incredible resource to the church. While the pastor can delegate some training, however, he cannot pass off the responsibility of developing leaders. Embracing this idea would radically change the expectations of both the pastor and the congregation.

LEADERS BECOME MISSIONARIES

There has been a shift in age demographics in missions. The average age of people joining our organization is the mid-30s. That is a change from several decades ago where young people graduated from Bible college and joined a mission agency the same month. Now it is typical for a graduate to consider missions a decade after the commencement service. This shift is a great opportunity to harmonize with the biblical model used for the first missionary journey. In Acts 13 where the church at Antioch launched missionaries, the recruiting pool was the leadership of the church. While today we may pick on the teens and suggest they should go into missions, at that time the Holy Spirit identified men who were already proven leaders.

Churches are full of young couples who could become missionaries. Perhaps we have failed to provide both the vision and the pathway from the pew to the mission field. It could be the pastor's role to identify and challenge potential missionaries.

It is also fascinating that the Holy Spirit did not communicate with the potential missionaries. He seemed to impress the other leaders or perhaps the congregation that Paul and Barnabas should be missionaries. What would happen if the church became sensitive to what God is doing in the lives of others and helped them determine God's direction for their lives? I've often said that mission agencies would like to get out of the recruiting business. That is the role of the church.

There are many middle-aged people who could become missionaries who wouldn't move to study at an institution. The great news is that there has never been a time in history where it is easier to bring the Bible college into the local church. That is why we need our institutions. They all have online deliverables that make the academic teaching readily available so that pastors can focus on spiritual development and ministry skills.

MENTORS CHOOSE PROTEGES

One of the challenges of this model of pastoring is that church members can be jealous if the pastor focuses on just a few. The pastor can be accused of having favorites. The expectation is that the pastor is there for everyone, and each member deserves equal attention. Pastors should not succumb to this criticism and simply follow in the footsteps of Jesus where He picked 12 and did not give equal time to everyone.

The principle is that the mentor chooses the protégé, not the other way around. Jesus did not accept volunteers. He picked the men He was going to disciple after a night of prayer. When volunteers came His way, He put up obstacles to send them away. This principle is true of many of the mentoring relationships we read in the Bible: Moses chose Joshua. Elijah chose Elisha. Barnabas chose Paul. Paul chose

Timothy. Therefore, it is the pastor's role to identify high potential people to train.

THE THRESHOLD OF FAITHFULNESS

The next issue to resolve is how a pastor can choose in whom to invest. The answer is "faithfulness." The pastor has a stewardship to invest in faithful men: "*and what you have heard from me in the presence of many witnesses entrust to faithful men, who will be able to teach others also*" (2 Timothy 2:2).

Faithfulness has been a primary character trait of many people of God:

> *Now Moses was* **faithful** *in all God's house as a servant, to testify to the things that were to be spoken later (Hebrews 3:5).*

> *So then, those who are of faith are blessed along with Abraham, the man of* **faith** *(Galatians 3:9).*

> *I thank him who has given me strength, Christ Jesus our Lord, because he judged me* **faithful***, appointing me to his service (1 Timothy 1:12).*

> *By Silvanus, a* **faithful** *brother as I regard him, I have written briefly to you, exhorting and declaring that this is the true grace of God. Stand firm in it (1 Peter 5:12).*

> *So that you also may know how I am and what I am doing, Tychicus the beloved brother and*

Logically, you don't want to train unfaithful men for ministry. It would be better to train one man who is faithful than 100 men who are unfaithful. Since faithfulness is so important, how do you know whether a person is faithful? Fortunately, Jesus gave us a test for that.

According to this passage, there are three ways you can identify faithful people:

1. Are they faithful in little things? This makes sense. No one becomes the CEO of a Fortune 500 company right out of college. The corporate ladder is designed to eliminate those who are not faithful. In Matthew 25:23 Jesus was talking about people who had been entrusted with talents. The basic principles is: *Well done, good and faithful servant. You have been faithful over a little; I will set you over much.* Faithfulness is an objective, observable

characteristic of an individual who consistently fulfills the small assignments.

2. Are they faithful in handling finances? This, too, is objective and easy to measure. How do they handle debt? Do they give to the church? Are they generous? Do they waste money? Are they in financial bondage? Do they pay their bills on time? Do they pay their taxes?

3. Are they faithful with other people's property? One of the big challenges employers have is finding people who will treat the company property like their own. I remember hearing of the owner of a McDonald's restaurant who would set up a test for those he was going to hire. Minutes before the applicant arrived for the interview, the owner would scatter trash in the parking lot. He would then watch to see if he or she would pick up the papers. He hired those who did.

If an individual does not demonstrate faithfulness in these three areas, then don't train him for leadership. I can speak from personal experience that it doesn't work. I regret violating this principle and then watching shipwrecks as unfaithful men crash on the rocks of ministry. If a person is not faithful, he is still back at the basic discipleship stage of his spiritual growth.

It is true that a pastor is pulled in multiple directions to satisfy the hopes and expectations of the congregation, but ultimately, he must stop trying to please everyone and start developing leaders. A pastor may eventually get the church to fulfill the Great Commission, but he is on a detour if he hasn't put training leaders in his job description. Imagine the accelerated speed of sending missionaries if a pastor could stay on the main highway without a detour.

REASON #2: INEXPERIENCE AT MENTORING

The second reason pastors gave for not Identifying, training and sending out tomorrow's missionaries is that they have never seen it done. It didn't happen in the church where they grew up, and it wasn't modeled in seminary where giving lectures was the primary approach to instruction. Thus, the major focus of ministry for some pastors revolves around the lectern and pulpit. The majority of the pastor's work week is spent in his study preparing the next lesson.

Before diagnosing any problem, it is beneficial to have a model of what is the ideal. If we don't know what could and should be, we could be on a detour and not even know it. The church at Antioch in the first century gives us a portrait of what could be the ideal. A model is just that—a model. This is what might be. It doesn't mean that every church needs to look just like this, but it gives us an idea of what could be. The narrative passages in scripture don't establish our theology, but they certainly illustrate it. Here is what scripture says about the sending of Paul and Barnabas as missionaries.

Now there were in the church at Antioch prophets and teachers, Barnabas, Simeon who was called Niger, Lucius of Cyrene, Manaen a lifelong friend of Herod the tetrarch, and Saul. While they were worshiping the Lord and fasting, the Holy Spirit said, "Set apart for me Barnabas and Saul for the work to which I have called them." Then after fasting and praying they laid their hands on them and sent them off (Acts 13:1-4).

There are several key thoughts that surface from this story:

1. When God chose missionaries, He went to the local church. It has been the practice of mission agencies to recruit primarily from Bible colleges and seminaries. While this makes sense, since these institutions are preparing people for ministry, it overlooks the fact that the local church is the way God is conducting His business on planet earth today. We highly value colleges and seminaries, but they are meant to be a support and supplement to the mission and vision of the church. While it may be simplistic to observe that missionaries come from a local church, the implications are profound when that idea is truly embraced. What if the local church took ownership of the identifying, equipping and sending of missionaries? While training institutions may be part of the process, it is not their responsibility to produce, commission and have a lifelong partnership with missionaries. What a difference it could make if the church made it a primary objective to identify, train and launch Great Commission workers from their congregation.

2. When God chose missionaries, He chose them from the leadership of the church. Traditionally, the path of most missionaries to the field was Bible college and then the mission field. While there were younger men like Timothy and Titus on

Paul's mission team, the primary responsibility for missions was on the backs of key leaders from the church. What a difference it could make if the church were looking to send proven, disciple-making leaders from their church instead of picking on the teens. Sending out young adults who are not deeply entrenched in the life of the church is a bit easier than sending out your key leaders. Sending out the right people will cause your church to suffer when they go. Barnabas and Paul were experienced teachers who had been pouring into that church for a year.

3. When God chose missionaries, He did so from a vibrant church. Acts 11:21 says this about the church: *And the hand of the Lord was with them, and a great number who believed turned to the Lord.* Verse 24 adds to this that *a great many people were added to the Lord.* There was so much work to be done that Barnabas recruited Paul to help: *So Barnabas went to Tarsus to look for Saul, and when he had found him, he brought him to Antioch. For a whole year they met with the church and taught a great many people* (25-26). There was a lot going on at this church. Evangelism was part of their DNA. While we cannot control the results from preaching the gospel, leadership is responsible for teaching and training the congregation to be hyper-active in outreach. It was out of this milieu of ministry that God launched the first missionaries.

4. When God chose missionaries, He did so from a praying church. It was during the 18th century that Zinzendorf brought renewal to that group of churches and started a movement that became

one of the greatest surges of missions in church history. The backdrop to that story is that they had a round-the-clock prayer meeting that lasted 100 years. The history of missions movements has frequently been preceded by prayer. The church at Antioch was characterized not only by prayer but also fasting. There was a seriousness that took away their appetite or at least the priority of eating.

5. When God chose missionaries, He used others to affirm their call which may have already taken place (Acts 9:15; 22:10, 14, 21 and 26:15-18). It is striking to notice that God did not communicate to the missionaries at this time since He had already called them. Scripture says: *The Holy Spirit said, Set apart for me Barnabas and Saul for the work to which I have called them* (Acts 13:2). The passage doesn't say whether it was the congregation or only the leadership that sensed this direction of the Holy Spirit, but it is obvious that He was not speaking to Paul and Barnabas. This is counterintuitive to an individualistic culture. If I'm supposed to be a missionary, I want the chill going down my back—not yours. What if the entire congregation viewed themselves as recruiters? Might there be more missionaries if the leadership of the church were sensitive to observing the work of God in the lives of leaders who might become missionaries?

The church at Antioch was obviously unique. Perhaps we cannot perfectly replicate it, but maybe there are some of these five elements that could be reproduced in our churches. Perhaps if you were doing what the church at Antioch was doing, your church could be a catalyst for launching missionaries.

Using this as a template, a church could then come up with a strategy to launch its own missionaries. It may be true that the pastor has never seen this before, but that is the joy of ministry. We should always be attempting to do things we have never done before. This is part of our lifelong learning.

I still remember the terror that struck my heart when I came to the realization that I needed to focus on just a few men to train them. As an introvert, I was far more comfortable being in the pulpit than conversing one-on-one across a coffee table. I was able to prepare for the pulpit and keep a professional distance, but mentoring required spontaneity, transparency, vulnerability, and personal relationships. Despite my fears, I was able to learn how to do this, and I assure you that if I can do it, anyone can do it.

REASON #3: NO MEN

A pastor may wish to train leaders, but what if he doesn't have men to train? There may be men in the church, but none of them seem to have leadership potential. It is not unusual that 60% of a congregation are women. In some places around the world the statistic is closer to 90%.

We have probably underestimated the potential and value of women in missions. This book is written to pastors and how they can personally mentor men, so I will not address the issue of women in missions, but we need to recognize the incredible accomplishments of women in missions. Ladies have made a major contribution to the fulfillment of the Great Commission, and in some instances accomplished more than men. Since it wouldn't be appropriate for a pastor to have the same kind of mentoring relationship with women in the church that he can have with the men, the following remarks are aimed at developing men.

There are many books written about why men don't go to church. These books identify issues that feminize Christianity that are a turn-off to men such as the church building décor, music, words to music, holding hands, and touchy-feely sermons. These books plea for a cause-driven, high-risk, bold-leadership kind of Christianity. Music that emphasizes strength and dynamic commitment. Preaching that calls men to battle. This is not a new issue to the church. In the 1800s, Charles Spurgeon said, "There has got abroad a notion, somehow, that if you become a Christian you must sink your manliness and turn milksop" (Murrow, 2011). It is still a topic that needs to be addressed but is beyond the scope of this book.

A MANLY FAITH

Paul does call for a manliness to our faith: *Be watchful, stand firm in the faith, **act like men**, be strong* (1 Corinthians 16:13 KJV). There may indeed be some obstacles in your church that repulse men, and there may be value to changing some of those things. It is not that men are not going to church, they may just not be going to your church because of some of these issues. Ultimately, men are being reached, and they attend a wide variety of churches, so the problem may not be the externals of your church culture. So instead, this chapter will explore some other concepts.

PLEAD WITH GOD

The starting place for finding men to train is for the pastor to get intentional and intense in prayer for this. It almost seems trite to begin with prayer, but It is God who calls men into ministry, so the starting place is to beg God to allow you to be part of the process. Additionally, Jesus gave prayer as the one primary approach to recruiting workers: *And he said to them, "The harvest is plentiful, but the laborers are few. Therefore pray earnestly to the Lord of the harvest to send out laborers into his harvest"* (Luke 10:2). While we might employ various recruiting strategies for missions, the starting point and the main point in finding new workers is to pray. How that works and why it works remain a mystery, but that should not keep us from simply doing what Jesus said.

RIGHT IN FRONT OF ME

Think about this: what if you had to leave your church in three years, and the church had to hire your successor from within the congregation? Would there be a candidate? What would you be doing right now if you knew you were leaving in three years?

I remember a time in South Africa when I was planting a church that had grown to the point that I should starting planning to move on and have a local pastor take over. In my naiveté I had not thought of training the next pastor, so I started a search throughout the country for someone the church could call. I was replicating my experience in American churches where there are always hundreds of pastors looking for a change of ministry. I was frustrated because there were no ready-made pastors for that church in spite of all my searching. Finally, I came to the realization that the next pastor was sitting in the pew right in front of me every Sunday. That started a pastoral training program that brought him to the place of shepherding the church so I could move on.

I tell that story because, like me, you may be looking right over the heads of potential leaders. The problem is that we can't always envision certain people in leadership. If we had been in charge of picking the 12 disciples for Jesus, we probably would not have picked any that Jesus did. The lesson here is that there may be more potential in your church than you think.

UNLIKELY

Paul gave us a baseline from which to work. He said:

> *Brothers and sisters, think of what you were when you were called. Not many of you were wise by human standards; not many were influential; not many were of noble birth. But God chose the foolish things of the world to shame the wise; God chose the weak things of the world to shame the strong. God chose the lowly things of this world and the despised things—and the things that are not—to nullify the things that are, so that no one may boast before him* (1 Corinthians 1:26-29).

God chooses leaders differently than the secular world. We need to get real. Most of us are surprised that God chose us to be church leaders. You may be surprised to discover a leader that is right in front of you every week.

ILLOGICAL

We were on a vision trip with several pastors and people interested in Indonesia. After several days together, one man indicated that there was no way he could envision being a missionary. He was committed to helping others and had a growing burden for this country but could not imagine that he was missionary material. I told him that he had just met the first criteria for being a missionary. All of us were at one time innocently sitting in a pew with no intention or aspiration of ever going into ministry. The fact that he could not envision it meant that he had just met the first qualification. There are those in your church right now who have no intention of being a church leader, but the work and grace of God may surprise you. So the first principle is to look beyond what is logical.

CORE INGREDIENTS

The next issue to consider is how to identify the raw material. In other words, how do you determine who has leadership potential? To a potter, it is not merely mud. In this untidy heap of dirt, the artist can see all the potential we overlook. To him it is a beautifully fashioned vase, alive with colors and patterns. Often, the same situation exists in training leaders. We need to see the potential in men who are right in front of us.

Previously we stated that the first and most important quality to look for is faithfulness. Paul said, *Now it is required that those who have been given a trust must prove faithful* (1 Corinthians 4:2). He told Timothy to find *reliable people who will also be qualified to teach others* (2 Timothy 2:2). He often referred to his co-workers as *faithful brothers*. As his own personal testimony, Paul said that God had *considered me trustworthy, appointing me to his service* (1 Timothy 1:12). Moses was characterized as *faithful* (Hebrews 3:1-6). God chooses people for leadership who are, first and foremost, faithful.

If a person is demonstrating faithfulness, then what else do you look for? The second quality is simply willingness. That is the first qualification of a church leader according to Paul: *Whoever **aspires** to be an overseer desires a noble task* (1 Timothy 3:4). The Greek word means *more than willing*; it means *craving or hungering for*. That raises the bar and makes it even more challenging to find a man of that mindset, but that is a good indicator that God is at work in the heart of a person. It isn't normal. That stirring may be the work of the Holy Spirit in his life. It is also the result of a person getting a taste of ministry.

The role of the pastor is to work in concert with God to identify those who could potentially be leaders. One of the approaches to this is to just start involving men in ministry. Provide ways for men to get a small taste of ministry. As hors d'oeuvres are to the main course of a meal, so too are small ministry opportunities. Here are some suggestions: reading scripture in a church service, leading in public prayer, accompanying the pastor to a hospital bed, praying with someone after a church service, giving their testimony. All these are small opportunities to whet a man's appetite for more ministry.

As already mentioned, it is the role of the mentor to choose protégés. The assumption is that there is a difference between discipleship and leadership training. Matthew 28:19-20 defines discipleship as training people *to observe* the commands of Christ. It is helping new believers to grow in Christ and become high-functioning followers of Jesus. In contrast, 2 Timothy 2:2 seems to be aimed at developing leaders. This passage is referring to those who will be able to develop others. There is a difference between new-believer discipleship and leadership training. Every newborn babe in Christ gets to be discipled, but not everyone should be trained as a leader. Every new Christian needs a spiritual parent, but not all Christians warrant the time and attention of a pastor to develop them as leaders.

FLAVORING HIS THINKING

It is the role of a pastor to be proactive in recruiting trainees. It could be as simple as the pastor making an appointment to talk with a man in the church. The conversation could go something like this:

> I've noticed that you are a faithful person. You are committed to fulfilling any tasks here around the church. You are someone who can be trusted to get things done. That is the major qualification for a leader, so I recognize your character and see your potential. I believe that God can use you in ways you have not yet imagined, and I would like to walk with you in exploring what that might be. Would you be willing to meet with me once a week to talk, study and pray and let's see where this goes?

Obviously, a negative response puts a stop to the idea, but you should assume that "no" simply means "no for now." This may be not be an idea that he has considered before. He may not be able to imagine his own potential. He may need time to consider the request. Either way you can be assured that your affirmation and proposal will be a great encouragement, and he may just need time to process the idea that a pastor wants to give him focused attention.

This proposal should be couched in the concept that leadership is not a position. It may be a step too far in an initial conversation to tell someone that you want to train him to be a missionary and move to Africa. Leadership is a function long before it is a position. So your suggestion is to simply improve his ability to lead in general.

Is leadership something you can learn, or are there only born leaders? While there are a very few people who just have an innate capacity to lead, the majority of leaders are those who have learned how to lead. Leadership is not a gene or mystical experience; it is a set of observable skills that can be developed. Anyone can be trained as a leader; the only question is how many people one can lead and in what capacity.

HEAD, HANDS AND HEART

There are three areas that need attention as a pastor mentors a future leader: (1) what he knows, (2) what he does, and (3) who he is. He must know the scripture, develop ministry skills and grow in Christ. This forms the curriculum for leadership development. It means there will be time each week when you are in the Word together, studying theology and hermeneutics. It will mean that each week you will also do ministry together so that you can coach him in ministry skills. It will mean spending time each week talking about his walk with God.

COACH RATHER THAN CONTROL

In the book *Turn This Ship Around*, David Marquet tells how he was assigned to be the captain of the USS Santa Fe, the worst submarine in the Navy. The miserable morale repulsed anyone who got a duty assignment to that tub. The book tells the story of how he turned this ship into one of the best and most coveted ships in the Navy.

The military has a clear command structure. It is assumed that a sailor's role is to obey the dictates of his superior. It is very much a command-and-control environment. However, Marquet started treating every sailor as a leader. Instead of waiting for orders, each sailor was treated as a leader who was responsible to figure out the next step. Obviously, there must be some kind of control on a ship, so everyone went to their leader and said, "I intend to . . ." In other words, each sailor was empowered to take command and come up with a plan for the next step, yet provided accountability so that a wrong decision didn't sink the ship. The genius was that everyone was assumed to be a leader.

One of the things that squelches leadership in a church is a pastor who has to be in charge and feels he needs to make every decision. Increasing the capacity to have leaders demands that the present leaders change from a control stance to empowerment. Changing your leadership style to that of David Marquet may just surface a plethora of potential leaders.

REASON #4: VISION

When we asked church leaders in our think tank why pastors don't train and send missionaries, an additional reason given was they just didn't have the aspiration to do so. The pastor or church may not have a vision for doing anything outside of their local church. If the pastor doesn't have his eyes on the world beyond his own city, he won't see the need to send missionaries from his congregation.

MISSIONAL OR ATTRACTIONAL

Foundational to a church being a sending church is a centrifugal movement that thrusts the focus of the church outward. It takes deliberate energy to reverse the default direction for a church which is centripetal, or inward-focused. In the Old Testament, Israel's stance was: We are here as a light. You must come and see us to learn about the glory of the one true God. We have special leaders and a building that is the house of the Lord. Come and join us. The New Testament completely reversed this concept. Instead of *come*, the operative word was *go*. The church may continue to operate on the Old Testament model, however. Instead of inviting nonbelievers to visit the church building, the church needs to launch itself into the world. The emphasis is on go-and-tell more than come-and-see. Every Christian is a believer-priest, mixing with nonbelievers in the marketplace and moving cross-culturally where the glory of God is in them, not in a building.

When a church creates great programs for every age and demographic, there is a tendency to increasingly pull the congregation into the vortex that creates a consumerism that we intrinsically reject. Centrifugal force is caused by a vision outside yourself. There must be a larger cause that focuses on others, or there is no need to be a sending church.

VISIONEERING

Shepherds are fantastic at caring for the sheep. Sheep like calmness and sameness, not excitement and change. For this reason, being visionary is not the intrinsic trait of the average pastor. Pastors tend to be managers, not leaders. They are exceptional at guarding, feeding and supporting the congregation but not necessarily setting goals and articulating a major vision for the church. Seminaries train pastors to exegete a passage and prepare a good sermon but spend little time on the subject of biblical leadership. That is ironic since shepherds are called upon to provide direction and to keep the sheep moving in paths of righteousness to new pastures.

It is all right if the pastor has management skills and is not visionary. He doesn't have to be able to do everything, and it is likely there are those in the church who are wired that way who could help set the direction for the church. The manager type shepherd would do well to gather together the visionary big-picture thinkers of the congregation to help create and drive the outward direction of the church. No matter who does it, someone must articulate and activate a vision.

THE TARGET

Good time management requires that there must be a target out there in the future. The basic principle is to set up the target first, then aim. Once there is a bull's-eye, then string the bow, pull the arrow out of the quiver, nock the arrow, draw the string and let it fly. There is no reason to perform all those actions if there is no bull's-eye. That is why casting vision is the first step. The place to start is with the end in mind.

THE FLOW

Another way to illustrate setting priorities and managing time is a waterfall. The water in the pool at the bottom cascades from the top. How do we decide what we should do in the next hour? That is governed by what needs to be accomplished today. How do we know what to do today? That is guided by what needs to be accomplished this week. This week's priorities flow from monthly goals, which flow from annual aspirations which ultimately come from right at the top of the waterfall which is the overall vision. There is no pool below if there is no waterfall above.

All of this distills to one simple idea: If a pastor has a vision for training and deploying missionaries from the church, it will happen. If that idea is not at the top of the waterfall, it will not be in the pool at the bottom. There is nothing mystical or magical here. It is as uncomplicated as the fact that training leaders is a big deal to the pastor.

FOCUSING A MISSIONAL TARGET

How would a pastor begin to cast vision for international ministries? Here is one approach. In the missions world, an unreached people group (UPG) is a cluster of people with a common language having less than 2% of that population claiming to be Christian. This is considered to be the tipping point where that church could potentially evangelize the rest of their group. Missiologists also talk about un-engaged people groups such as a language population in which there is no active church planting taking place. Both groups need help from outside to create a church planting movement.

Estimates vary that there are between 6,000 and 7,000 of these language groups that are still unreached. Because these exist, we have not yet completed the Great Commission, which includes taking the gospel to every person on earth.

This framework makes it simple for a pastor to cast vision for that local church. Why not take on the responsibility of one of these groups? It is measurable. It is easily defined. The average believer can get excited about taking the gospel to those who have never heard.

Some churches have an ambition to support a missionary in every country in the world. They want pins on every region of the map in the church foyer. It is, however, expecting too much for the congregation to focus on 180 different places around the world. Narrowing the church's ambitions to only a few specific targets will concentrate and intensify interest and awareness. One local church cannot reach the whole world, but they can do something. It is the role of leadership to identify those places. This is a reason why pastors need to visit the mission field.

VISION TRIPS

It is estimated that evangelical churches spend over $2 billion a year in short-term trips. Imagine the difference it would make if that money were spent on sending church leaders to the mission field instead of teens? What if pastors became the chief missiologists of the church? What if pastors knew where in the world the needs exist and could speak intelligently and passionately about a specific people group?

This is why it ought to be part of the missions budget to regularly send the pastor overseas. These are vision trips and need not be ministry trips. Rather, pastors are scouting the world to identify and adopt unfilled gaps in the Great Commission and learn about international ministry.

No business would start a branch office or build a new factory in a place that the management had never visited. Due diligence is to visit the place and determine the viability of extending their business to that location. In the same way, the pastor and church leaders should scout the land to determine where they might want to start a remote ministry. Vision flows from the pulpit. The heart of the pastor shows up in his sermons and what he talks about on a regular basis.

In *Gaining by Losing,* J D. Greear describes how their church became a sending church. One chapter heading is "Your Church Doesn't Need a Missions Pastor." Larger churches with multiple staff members often designate one of those assistant pastors to lead the missions outreach. Greear argues that the senior pastor ought to be that missions pastor. The reason is that missions is the mission of the church. The main thing the church should be doing is the Great Commission, so this shouldn't be delegated to someone else. Missions is not the concern of a few cloistered in a committee; it should be the over-all consuming occupation of the church. Everything it does and every program it runs should contribute directly to preparing the church to reach the world.

MISSION—THE REASON WHY

This discussion raises a topic that we should address before talking about a vision, and that is the subject of "mission." Many would use this as a synonym for "purpose." Regardless of the term you prefer to use, it is important to ask the question WHY the church exists. Vision speaks to the topic of WHERE the church is headed; but before that, there must be a clear understanding of the WHY.

Most churches have a mission or purpose statement, yet few in the church could tell you what it is. Many pastors could not quote it even though it is one of the first statements in the church constitution. Many church purpose statements are so long and complicated that few will ever memorize it. It was created at the formation of the church and then promptly forgotten. It may be beneficial to dust off the mission statement and update the wording.

MISSION, VALUES, VISION

Returning to the waterfall illustration . . . the river that flows to the top of the waterfall is the mission statement. Before the water starts cascading over the cliff, there is a river that feeds the cascade. That river is the mission and a list of the values of the church which leads to the vision and ultimately the strategy. Strategy is the final part of the journey before the water plunges into the pool. Strategy is simply how everything else is going to be accomplished. It is the "how to" of getting it done. Unfortunately, many churches start with strategy and keep going through the motions without looking above them to mission, values and vision. Day-to-day activities are accomplished with great fervor with disregard to the top of the waterfall and the river that leads to it. Casting vision must flow from the mission and values.

This is not just an academic exercise. Unless a church simply wants to go through the motions and flail away at programs and events, they must do the hard work of articulating mission, values and mission. By definition, a leader has an idea of where he is going and what is the preferred future. The flip side is that a follower is someone who is coming along behind someone who knows where he is going. This is the role of a leader. He must know where he is headed. He must be dissatisfied with the status quo and see a better future. In this application, the pastor cannot accept that there is an unreached people group and can visualize a church in every village and town in that region. That aspiration then drives the need to train leaders and send missionaries.

This approach to leadership may be dismissed by relegating it to the business world, but the Apostle Paul conducted his ministry this way and explains his approach in Romans 15.

1. **He had a mission**: *leading the Gentiles to obey God* (18). He was the Apostle to the Gentiles, and his reason for existence—his "why"—was to evangelize Gentiles.

2. **He had values:** *It has always been my ambition to preach the gospel where Christ was not known* (20). While others stayed in Jerusalem, it was important for him to press into regions of the world that had not yet been exposed to the gospel.

3. **He had a vision**: *So from Jerusalem all the way around to Illyricum, I have fully proclaimed the gospel of Christ* (19). His goal was measurable. It was specific. He knew where he was going.

4. **He had a strategy:** *This is why I have often been hindered from coming to you. But now that there is no more place for me to work in these regions, and since I have been longing for many years to visit you, I plan to do so when I go to Spain. I hope to see you while passing through and to have you assist me on my journey there, after I have enjoyed your company for a while. Now, however, I am on my way to Jerusalem in the service of the Lord's people there* (22-25). Paul had a plan. He knew what he needed to do next.

In the middle of discussing his leadership role, Paul quotes a passage from Isaiah to argue the foundational basis of his vision. *Those who were not told about him will see, and those who have not heard will understand* (Romans 15:19). The principle here is that our ideas about the future must be based on scripture. The vision for the future must have a biblical basis. That simplifies things for a pastor. It doesn't take a wild imagination to come up with a plan for the future; it is simply putting feet to what God has already said. That means the leadership of a church merely needs to articulate how they are going to fulfill the Great Commission.

Here is a test: if we asked you right now to stand up and explain to your church the mission, values, vision and strategy of the church, could you do it? Could you do that in three minutes? If you could not, then there is a lot of work that needs to be done.

REASON #5: IGNORANCE

When pastors at the think tanks used the word *ignorance*, they were not referring to the IQ of shepherds. They were talking about a lack of knowledge and information. In other words, pastors who do not train leaders and launch missionaries didn't know that was something they were supposed to do or how to do it. There is an assumption that sending a missionary was a good thing if it happened, but pastors did not see this as an integral part of their job description.

As was already mentioned, a typical seminary education focuses on theology, exegesis and homiletics. The emphasis of western education is on content, not on skills development. In the Greek model of education, you can graduate because you acquired enough information. Grades are based on whether you passed the written test. It is possible to secure your degree from a Bible college but not know how to preach, evangelize, counsel, teach, perform weddings or funerals, lead a church or administrate communion. Our educational system focuses on the mind, not the heart or the ministry skills.

EFFECTIVE COMMUNICATORS BRING THEM IN

It is logical for pastors to pattern their church ministry after their seminary experience. In past years, the model of ministry was to "have a strong pulpit and they will come." If getting the pews filled is the ultimate goal, then it is a valid argument to have a compelling communicator in the pulpit. If the goal is primarily for people to have knowledge, then it is important to have a world-class teacher. Celebrity pastors are valued and are known for their communication skills because we value information.

Knowledge, however, is a steppingstone. It is not an end to itself. The purpose of knowing is in order to "do" not just to "know." James warned against just acquiring information without doing something with it:

> *Do not merely listen to the word, and so deceive yourselves. Do what it says. Anyone who listens to the word but does not do what it says is like someone who looks at his face in a mirror and, after looking at himself, goes away and immediately forgets what he looks like. But whoever looks intently into the perfect law that gives freedom, and continues in it—not forgetting what they have heard, but doing it— they will be blessed in what they do* (James 1:22-25).

Pride is an additional danger of merely acquiring knowledge without application. Paul puts it this way: *knowledge puffs up while love builds up* (1 Corinthians 8:1). Ministry appears easy in a classroom because it is just head knowledge, but things change immediately when you step into real life and have to do something with that knowledge. Preaching looks simple in the classroom, but stepping into a pulpit in a real church with a live audience quickly brings humility. It is easy to critique the preaching of others if I don't preach. Counseling may seem simple in a classroom, but it is radically different to actually help someone.

Gnosticism was fueled by a pride of those who knew compared to those who didn't know. It created a hierarchical elitism. It glorified the cognitive. Robes, lecterns, and raised platforms were tools to emphasize a professional distance between those "in the know" and those who had yet to learn. Gnosticism was an errant theology that led to pride and elevation above the masses.

EFFECTIVE MENTORS SEND THEM OUT

It has already been argued several times in this book that Ephesians 4:11-12 articulates one of the key components of the pastor's job description. In this passage the job description has to do with ministry skills, not knowledge.

The Western (or Greek) model of education revolves around knowledge in a formal, institutional setting. It is normally conducted in a classroom with a set curriculum, lectures that last 45 minutes, accreditation and finally graduation. The Eastern (or Hebrew) approach to education was that you were not considered educated unless you could do something with what you knew. Information was a pathway to being and doing. So while Greeks would ask questions about God to know the answers, the Hebrews ask questions about God to know Him.

Greeks would learn through listening, while Hebrews would learn by doing. For instance, if the goal is to teach about Mormonism, the Western approach would be to have a series of lectures. The Eastern model would tell the student to find a Mormon and seek to evangelize him. When that happens, the student immediately begins to understand what he doesn't know and is highly motivated to learn. Additionally, he is learning so that he can minister to someone, not just to get a good grade.

An example of the Eastern approach is when Paul grabbed Timothy at the beginning of his second missionary journey and invited him to accompany him. Education took place on the fly as they did ministry together. Instead of sending Timothy off to a Bible college in Jerusalem, he trained him in real life.

This illustrates another major difference. Western education is training *for* service, while Eastern education is training *in* service. Jesus opted for this approach with his disciples. He could have created a Bible college and spent three years lecturing. Instead, Jesus took them with Him as He did ministry. Periodically He would send them out on assignments. At times they would return rejoicing over success, but other times they came back humiliated by failure. The lecture would come after attempted ministry, not before. Jesus built no schools and did not participate in a lecture circuit. He simply chose 12 and ministered with them for 3 ½ years.

THE ACADEMY BEGAN WITH MENTORING

In the early days of the founding of our country, there were no schools. If someone wanted to become a pastor, he simply moved into the pastor's house and lived with him. They would have their devotions together in the morning, work on messages together during the day, talk theology over the dinner table, and visit parishioners together. Some of these pastors were better at mentoring than others, so the good ones got together and created Harvard and Princeton so they could do this full time. Since then, we have not looked back and have multiplied our learning institutions. This became an expensive approach to producing pastors since it required buildings, faculty salaries, libraries and utility bills. Pastoral mentoring comes at little additional cost since churches and pastors already have buildings, salaries, libraries and utility bills.

THE HEART AND HANDS SUPPLEMENT

Be assured that Bible colleges and seminaries should be highly valued and are a tremendous asset to the church. I am definitely not pushing against our institutions of learning. We greatly benefit from the scholarship and academic excellence. I am not arguing AGAINST formal institutions of education but rather arguing FOR adding local church training, pastoral mentoring. We need both; and it could be argued that if we did more church-based training, it would increase enrollment at brick-and-mortar colleges since we are building a learning culture into our churches.

The institution provides a great resource for the academic side of training the next generation, and with technology there has never been an easier way to import that part of education into the local church. The recent closure of multiple Bible colleges is a major loss to the advancement of missions and ministry in America. I am arguing for BOTH eastern and western education. This is a plea to pastors to recognize the value of the strategic nature of their participation in training people for ministry.

This is also an urging to do all three facets of training at the same time. In other words, it is not the head first, then at some time in the future focus on hands and heart. They all interact with each other in the educational process and should be done simultaneously. Approaching it otherwise is like sending a head off to college to sew it back on to the body to develop hands and heart later. There is a synergy that takes place when all three happen at the same time.

I remember a moment in one of our think tanks where a pastor came to the realization that if he accepted this idea, it would radically change his ministry. He confessed that the majority of his time was spent at a computer monitor. Training leaders would take him out of the office to do ministry side-by-side in real life with real people in real time. It may be that "I didn't know" is a valid excuse . . . until now.

MISSIO-IGNORANCE

There is a second facet to the ignorance issue. In addition to simply not knowing that training and sending missionaries is part of the job description, there is a lack of knowledge about missions in general. Missions-minded seminary profs have frequently grieved that it is next to impossible to get missions courses into the curriculum for pastoral training. Most Bible colleges require that those in the pastoral course take an introduction to missions course, but that is about all the formal education that takes place on the subject.

This is a bit incongruous since the Great Commission is the mission, the main agenda, of the church. It should be the outcome of local church ministry. It is the overall purpose of church ministry. It would seem that pastors would have an innate interest in this topic.

There are many theological and practical issues that pastors need to be aware of as they shepherd their churches. Missions has often been on the leading edge of theological rabbit trails and theological compromise. Much of the ecumenical movement has been driven by the missions world. Even something as simple and clear as the gospel is distorted or redefined first in the missions world. The topic of social justice was a huge issue in the missions world long before it reached the front pages of our theological discussions in the United States.

Topics like contextualization, indigenization, syncretism, ecclesiology, church planting and evangelism are all missions topics, but those same issues affect the sending church. One of the untapped resources for the home church is the experiences and expertise of the missionaries they send out. The leaders of the church in the book of Acts were the missionaries, yet we have relegated them to some lower position on the ecclesiastical ladder. The sending church needs missionaries and their pastor to be fully engaged in missions.

Fortunately, there is an overwhelming abundance of resources available to pastors who want to wrestle with missions issues. Some seminaries have filled the gap, and degree level work is now available on international ministries. There are major organizations like Missio Nexus that provide a plethora of resources for learning about missions and contemporary issues. Every pastor would benefit from subscribing to the

Evangelical Missions Quarterly. Thousands of books have been written about missions and missionary work. The Evangelical Missions Society provides conferences and resources that constantly wrestle with theological and practical issues in international ministries. With all these resources readily available, lack of opportunity is not a reason today for ignorance.

REASON #6: INSECURITY

I had just accepted the role of Director for a mission agency and knew that I was in way over my head. Bible college had not trained me to lead or manage a nonprofit organization. I knew a little about theology, exegesis, homiletics and apologetics. I knew how to plant a church and had been a part of three of those projects, but leading a mission agency was not something for which I was prepared. I did, however, know enough to seek seasoned leaders to mentor me. One of those men had been a director of another similar organization but was now serving as the administrative pastor for one of the most prestigious churches in town. There were far more millionaires per pew than almost any church in America.

My mentor mentioned one day that he was resigning from his role at this church because of the insecurities of the senior pastor who made life miserable for staff members. I remember being incredulous that a celebrity pastor of such a famous church could be insecure. My mentor insisted that most leaders are insecure. Henry Blackaby said, "I am convinced that there are more men in pastoral ministry motivated by insecurity rather than calling" (Leeman, 2017). This opinion is supported by those pastors in think tanks who said that insecurity was a reason for not producing leaders.

At the heart of insecurity is self-doubt, but leaders don't really want to betray those thoughts. They are supposed to know what they are doing and can't let others know what they are really feeling. Insecurity can manifest itself in all kinds of ways. Bravado creates an artificial boldness that shows up to strongly voice opinions. Insecure leaders might not ask for input from other people for fear that this might indicate weakness. Alternately, it might show up by silence because they fear being wrong. Or this might just be smug pride. Regardless of the motivations, there is a desire for self-preservation.

INVERSE PRIDE

Pride often drives insecurity, and by pride I mean self-focus and self-orientation. Insecure people are consumed with questions such as: What will others think of me? What if I look foolish? What if I am wrong? What will people say? All those questions are self-focused. They are about me. They spring from seeking to preserve an image of myself that is full of pride.

If my mentor is correct, one of the reasons pastors do not train leaders is insecurity. There are perhaps several reasons underlying this insecurity.

1. Pastors may fear that if they train people, someone else might do their job better than they can or that they may potentially replace them. We could call this "the King Saul complex" recalling how Saul felt enraged when he heard *Saul has slain his thousands, but David his tens of thousands* (1 Samuel 29:5). The reality is that there could be people in the church who are better speakers, better leaders, better teachers, better shepherds or better at almost all that pastors are called upon to do. A pastor can either ignore that

or provide a platform for these gifted people to minister. The secure leader must come to a point where he admits that the ministry is much bigger than himself.

2. Pastors may not want to be transparent enough to bring potential leaders close to them to adequately train them. Many pastors are introverts and like privacy. They don't really want someone looking over their shoulder. It is difficult to pull back the curtain of their devotional life, prayer habits, personal discipline and time management to let others see what they are really like. Insecurity seeks to establish a professional distance between the pulpit and the pew.

3. Pastors may not believe they have enough qualifications to train missionaries, especially compared to college and seminary profs. Since our primary view of education is knowledge-based, the average pastor may not think he has the academic qualifications or expertise to teach at that level. This belief emerges from the western, Greek model of education discussed earlier.

4. Another issue is that a pastor may not really know what he is doing so feels inadequate to pass on to others what he does not know. He can prepare and preach a sermon but may have never thought through how he does that. The truth is that most of us do our best work when we really don't know what we are doing. In those instances, we are assured that if anything results from our ministry, it was God that did it in spite of ourselves. Yet in our heart we know that we don't actually know what we are doing.

THE WAY DOWN IS THE WAY UP

The opposite of pride is humility, an others-oriented discipline that is actually just an act of obedience. Notice the imperatives: *Humble yourselves, therefore, under God's mighty hand, that he may lift you up in due time* (1 Peter 5:6). Additionally James writes: *Humble yourselves before the Lord* (James 4:10). Scripture says just do it. The key is to have a proper evaluation of ourselves. One of the classic sections of scripture on this topic is 1 Corinthians 1:26-31.

> *Brothers and sisters, think of what you were when you were called. Not many of you were wise by human standards; not many were influential; not many were of noble birth. But God chose the foolish things of the world to shame the wise; God chose the weak things of the world to shame the strong. God chose the lowly things of this world and the despised things—and the things that are not—to nullify the things that are, so that no one may boast before him. It is because of him that you are in Christ Jesus, who has become for us wisdom from God—that is, our righteousness, holiness and redemption. Therefore, as it is written: "Let the one who boasts boast in the Lord."*

The reality is that none of us amount to much. Why would we think so highly of ourselves when God has already stated that He has chosen the *foolish, weak and lowly*. Who do we think we are that we should have any pride? We have nothing to brag about.

Paul is probably referring to our salvation when he tells us to *consider your calling.* We are not *wise men* or *mighty* or *noble.* In other words, our brains, brawn or birth were not conditions to our salvation. It was all His grace. Others think that in this passage, Paul is referring to our calling to ministry. If that is the case, then we still don't have a reason for pride.

Jesus chose men who would not normally be candidates for such an important goal of starting and advancing the church. That group of disciples included rough fishermen without education, limited vocabulary and bad grammar (and probably bad language). Jews considered Matthew a mercenary who had sold his soul to a foreign government to collect taxes from his countrymen. Simon the Zealot was a revolutionary and potential terrorist. The Sons of Thunder were certainly not refined or dignified. Others identified this group as *unlearned and ignorant men* (Acts 4:13).

We are certainly not any better than the men Jesus chose for his Twelve. Jesus continues to choose the *foolish things of the world to confound the wise.* The word *foolish* comes from the word *moron*—obviously not a complimentary term and certainly not one we would want applied to ourselves. But get over it. We are ultimately moronic in comparison to the wisdom of God.

God has often used low potential people to do His work. Moses was a stuttering recluse who did everything possible to escape leadership responsibilities. Jonah was a racist escape artist with a bad attitude. David was just a kid. Gideon was the *least in his family's house* (Judges 6:15). Rahab was a harlot. The Apostle Paul wrote this about himself: *I came to you in weakness with great fear and trembling. My message and my preaching were not with wise and persuasive words, but with a demonstration of the Spirit's power, so that your faith might not rest on human wisdom, but on God's power* (I Corinthians 2:3–5). Paul's admission of inadequacy was his strength. Instead of a façade of bravado, he readily acknowledged his weakness and fear.

Ultimately, we can't accomplish anything anyway; it is God working in and through us. Jesus told us to look at it this way: *I am the vine; you are the branches. If you remain in me and I in you, you will bear much fruit;* **apart from me you can do nothing** (John 15:5).

The world around us also has a low view of those in ministry. MacArthur writes in his commentary on 1 Corinthians:

> In 178 AD the philosopher Celsus mockingly wrote of Christians: *"Let no cultured person draw near, none wise and none sensible, for all that kind of thing we count evil; but if any man is ignorant, if any man is wanting in sense and culture, if anybody is a fool, let him come boldly [to become a Christian]. . . . We see them in their own houses, wool dresses, cobblers, the worst, the vulgarest, the most uneducated persons. . . . They are like a swarm of bats or ants creeping out of their nest, or frogs holding a symposium around a swamp, or worms convening in mud"* (MacArthur, 1985).

At certain times in history, clergy were held in high esteem, but that was not always the case and is rarely true anymore.

NOTHING + GRACE = SOMETHING

On a certain level, it is healthy to have insecurities. When we recognize we are not capable of producing results, we are in a good place. After the resurrection, Peter went back to fishing. Although he was a professional fisherman, he couldn't catch any fish until Jesus came along and told him how to do it. Our natural abilities may cause us to think we can muscle our way through ministry for some semblance of success. As we kneel at the foot of the cross and begin to grasp grace, there is no response but to fall on our faces, admit our insecurities and wait to see God do above and beyond our imagination.

The solution to insecurity is to admit our inadequacies, take on a posture of humility and admit we don't really amount to much. That level of transparency will allow us to let future leaders into our private lives. Our insecurities should never be an obstacle to training.

REASON #7: TIME

Pastors are notoriously over-worked. For many, a 40-hour work week would seem like a vacation. Many find it difficult to take a day off; and even if they do, they are answering phone calls, text messages and email. They cut many vacations short to return for a funeral or parishioner in need. So it seems outlandish to suggest that a pastor should devote another 20 hours a week to training leaders. It would be extremely difficult to add leadership training to their job description.

SUBSTITUTION NOT ADDITION

The solution is not to work more hours. Time is not elastic. Part of the answer is "instead of" rather than "in addition to." The answer is to change the pastor's job description. The answer is shifting priorities.

Ephesians 4:11-12 is one of the key passages for the job description of a pastor:

> *So Christ himself gave the apostles, the prophets, the evangelists, the pastors and teachers, to equip his people for works of service, so that the body of Christ may be built up.*

According to this passage, the main role of leadership is to train others to do ministry. Regardless of how you define *apostles, prophets, evangelists* and *shep-*

herd/teachers, they are all leadership positions, and it is clear that those out front should be developing others to do what they do.

The word *equip* has the idea of training. Nida says that the word means "to make someone completely adequate or sufficient for something—'to make adequate, to furnish completely, to cause to be fully qualified, adequacy'" (Louw & Nida, 1966). This confronts our current model of pastoral ministry. God gives leaders to local churches to make sure that believers are furnished, sufficient and qualified to do ministry. The focus is that the congregation has skills based on knowledge, not simply knowledge. There is something out of kilter when a pastor has been there a decade, and men in the church cannot run a basic home Bible study, or he wouldn't trust them to do so.

DO AND TRAIN

What is the job description of an evangelist? It seems logical to say that it's to do evangelism. After all, that is the gift. It seems to come easy to the evangelist, and he is good at it, so we would assume his role is to be out there doing evangelism 60 hours a week. But that is not what the text says. This is the only place in scripture that gives the ministry description of an evangelist, and clearly his role is to *equip saints to do the work of the ministry*. In other words, train others to do evangelism.

Paul told Timothy to *do the work of an evangelist* (2 Timothy 4:5). We might assume that Paul was telling his protégé to get out there and do some evangelism. Yet Ephesians 4:11-12 makes it clear that Paul was telling Timothy to train others in evangelism. The work of an evangelist is to train others. Evangelists do evangelism because they are Christians, not because they are evangelists. Every believer should be engaged in the Great Commission, so we need evangelists to train and motivate everyone to get involved.

In the same way, it is the role of a pastor to train others to do what he is good at. The pastor may be gifted in teaching, counseling, showing mercy, encouraging, visiting the sick and comforting the bereaved. He should be training others to do those things so that he doesn't have to do all of it by himself. His job description is to do ministry AND to train others to do that same type of ministry.

THE EXPONENTIAL EFFECT

One of the reasons pastors work so hard is because they have not trained others to do ministry. It is logical that more work can be done if more people are doing it. More people will not do it until leaders take the time to equip them to minister. Jesus said that *everyone who is fully trained will be like their teacher* (Luke 6:40). Taking the time and making the effort to train others to do ministry means there are others who can do what you do.

One of the basic characteristics of leaders is that they make things happen. Leaders are doers. They accomplish things. They get things done. So if things are not happening, perhaps one of the solutions is to have more leaders. If you don't have leaders, and you have been in your present ministry role for a year, that is understandable; but if you have been in your present ministry for ten years and there are not enough leaders, that is your fault. Your job is to train leaders.

There are some wonderful outcomes for the pastor who focuses on training others to minister. Ephesian 4:11-12 gives the job description, and the following verses outline what will happen when leaders train others.

1.   Saints will be equipped to do ministry (4:12).
2.   Saints will serve (4:12).
3.   Churches will be built (4:12).
4.   Churches will be unified (4:13).
5.   Saints will know God (4:13).
6.   Saints become mature (4:13).
7.   Saints know scripture (4:14).
8.   Saints are loving (4:15).
9.   Churches are fully functional (4:16).

Wouldn't it be wonderful if you could describe your church with those nine characteristics? Who would not want a church that looks like that? The pathway for this to happen is through developing others to do the work of the ministry.

One of the keys to time management is to do only what only you can do. If someone else can do it, then delegate. If that maxim is true, then training leaders is something that only leaders can do. Followers will not train leaders. Only leaders can train leaders. So leadership training is not something that can be handed off to others. The pastor must commit to mentoring the next generation. Seminaries commonly train pastors to spend 25-30 hours a week preparing their Sunday morning message. If there are more weekly teaching responsibilities, is it realistic that a pastor can fulfill his job description (Ephesians 4:11-12) if he spends all his time in the office getting ready to preach the next sermon? Training leaders will require rewriting your job description.

NEVER WORK ALONE

There is another concept that needs to be factored into this situation. The key to leveraging your time is never to work alone. It is not really the issue of carving out an additional 20 hours a week to do leadership training. The key is to include others in what you are already doing. You are going to prepare a message anyway, so why not have someone looking over your shoulder? You are going to make a hospital visit, so why not take someone with you? You're going to do counseling, so why not have a trainee in the room with you? The solution is not that you need to have more time to devote to leadership training. Rather, the key is to use the time you already have designated for ministry by including others. It obviously will take a little bit longer to bring someone else along since there will need to be discussion and debriefing, but it is not like devoting all of your time to only doing leadership development. You can do two things at once.

FIX THE LEAKING CALENDAR

Another concept that a pastor could consider is improving his own personal time management. Not many of us could claim to have this facet of our life in total array. There's always room for improvement. Chances are you have a lot more hours available to you than you think. You might want to figure out why you struggle in this area or at least take a course or read some books on time management.

We do not tend to value our time like we should. Attorneys keep track of their billable hours in six-minute increments. Even though you as a pastor are not paid by the hour, what if you placed a value of $1000 an hour on your time? Would it make a difference in how you spent the next six minutes?

One of the most important biblical concepts to understand for time management is the difference between *chronos* and *kairos*. In my book *Chief*, I write at length about this topic:

> There are two Greek words for time. **Chronos** is the word that refers to minutes, hours, and days. It is the normal word we use for time. **Kairos** is something different. It carries the idea of capitalizing on an opportunity. Time management in Western cultures tends to focus on *chronos*. They are concerned with how to put more minutes in the day—or at least do more in the minutes available. While that may be important, good time management is concerned with both *chronos* and *kairos*. (Seger, Chief, 2013)

Scripture uses both of those words, sometimes in the same sentence. For instance, Jesus said: *It is not for you to know times* [chronos] *or seasons* [kairos] *that the Father has fixed by his own authority* (Acts 1:7).

Chronos is our default approach to time management. Since most of us understand scheduling minutes and hours, we should concentrate more on the *kairos*. Investors are balancing these two concepts all the time. We know that investment in our 401k works well with cost dollar averaging . . . just consistently investing money month after month and ignoring the direction of the markets. It takes an expert to figure out when is a good time to get in and when to get out of the market. That is *kairos*. It is looking for those excellent opportunities that will produce giant returns.

Further, in my book *Chief*, I write:

> There is a story in the Bible about anti-Semitism. The entire nation of Israel was threatened with extermination. Esther happened to be in the right place at the right time. She had access to the king to plead the case for the preservation of her countrymen. Her cousin Mordecai encouraged her to be bold. He framed the context of her situation by pointing out that perhaps she was in this position *for such a time as this* (Esther 4:14). That was *kairos*. She had that golden opportunity that would never present itself again. She could either take advantage of it or lose it forever. (Seger, Chief, 2013)

Training leaders requires both kinds of time. It requires setting out a calendar and schedule to meet with potential leaders to train. It is grinding out a schedule, relentlessly, day after day and week after week, but it also requires sensitivity to *kairos* time. There will be teachable moments. People may now be available to be trained that were not ready last year. There are phases in a person's life when God is working in his heart to be more receptive to the idea of ministry leadership. Whereas you could have talked to him last year about being a leader and he would not have been interested, things have changed in his life and now he is ready. It takes a pastor aware of *kairos* to capitalize on the current openness of potential leaders.

Being sensitive to *kairos* means that you will move aside some of the things on your schedule. While we need to plan a calendar, there are times when those plans should be set on a shelf to take advantage of a golden opportunity. Living by *chronos* with a well-organized schedule means that we are better positioned to take advantage of opportunities when they come our way.

We may use lack of time as a reason for not training leaders, but the reality is we have not made it a priority. This book is a compilation of all the reasons pastors gave for not training missionaries in their church. Ultimately, however, there is one reason why churches don't produce missionaries: the pastor doesn't want to. Churches that are major sending churches seem to have the common denominator that the pastor wants it to happen. The church may not have systems in place to make it happen, but because it is a heart desire of the pastor, it happens. Even though time management is an important issue, it is not the main issue. Desire is.

J. D. Greear says it well:

> What your organization does best grows out of what it loves most. To send effectively, we must love the glory of God and the lost more than we love anything else. Then sending comes naturally.

> Our problem is not that we haven't found the right program that enables us to reach the

world. Our problem is that we don't yearn to see God's glory spread over the earth enough to build whatever ships are required to reach people for Christ and see his glory awakened in their heart (Greear, Gaining by Losing: Why the Future Belongs to Churches That Send, 2015).

REASON #8: COST

To train and send a missionary from your church will cost you in at least two ways. First, you will be losing a key leader. Second, you will be financially supporting someone who was previously a financial giver. That makes it a double hit. There is a price to pay.

My first ministry after Bible college was to serve as an assistant pastor in a church in North Carolina. That was a wonderful experience, and God blessed richly. To this day there are people who fondly remember those days of ministry. When I joined an agency and headed to South Africa as a missionary, the church took on half of my support. The irony was that half of my support as a missionary was more than my salary as an assistant pastor. Sending me away actually cost the church more than if I had stayed.

There are two issues that factor into the high cost of sending a missionary.

First, the missionary must raise support for everything that an employer would normally pay. He furnishes his own office, pays the entirety of Social Security taxes, sometimes pays taxes in two countries and covers his own ministry expenses. There are no 401k matching contributions. In other words, he is a self-contained "business" that must provide everything for both the family and the ministry. Normally only about half of the support schedule is salary.

Secondly, the cost of living overseas is often greater than in the States. There was a day when a missionary left for Africa with only a rifle, a pith helmet and a Bible. Those days are over. In many countries around the world, the cost of living is higher than living in downtown New York City. In some countries the cost of living index is four times as high as the United States. There was a time when most missionaries lived in rural settings. You could grow, catch or shoot your food, but most of the world's population has moved to the city. Cities are expensive. Add all of this to the weakening dollar and inflation rates of 15-20% in some countries around the world, and you have a recipe for high support schedules.

According to the Harvard Business Review,

> On average, expatriates cost two to three times what they would in an equivalent position back home. A fully loaded expatriate package including benefits and cost-of-living adjustments costs anywhere from $300,000 to $1 million annually (The Right Way to Manage Expats, 1999).

From that vantage point, missionaries operate at bargain basement prices, yet the price tag on missions is extremely high.

In addition to the financial cost, the loss of key leaders for your church is a high price to pay. The assumption is that anyone who is a missionary should first qualify as a church leader (1 Timothy 3). In other words, this is a key person in your church, and when he leaves for the mission field, he will be missed. If he will not be missed, you should not send him. It cost the church at

Antioch dearly to let go of Paul and Barnabas. There is no way around the fact that training missionaries and sending them is a costly endeavor.

Jesus made it abundantly clear that following Him was going to cost something.

> *As they were walking along the road, a man said to him, "I will follow you wherever you go."*
>
> *Jesus replied, "Foxes have dens and birds have nests, but the Son of Man has no place to lay his head."*
>
> *He said to another man, "Follow me."*
>
> *But he replied, "Lord, first let me go and bury my father."*
>
> *Jesus said to him, "Let the dead bury their own dead, but you go and proclaim the kingdom of God."*
>
> *Still another said, "I will follow you, Lord; but first let me go back and say goodbye to my family."*
>
> *Jesus replied, "No one who puts a hand to the plow and looks back is fit for service in the kingdom of God"* (Luke 9:57-62).

God's way comes with an expensive price tag. We shouldn't be surprised when missions dig into our resources.

The issue of the high cost of missions has led some to jettison the traditional model of supporting American missionaries to supporting nationals in other countries around the world. The idea is to find someone "over there" and financially support them instead of sending someone from America. The rationale is that you can hire four nationals for the price of sending one American, and the national already knows the language and culture, so they will be more effective. This sounds logical, but let's look at this idea.

1. We cannot buy our way out of the Great Commission. For an affluent country like America, the easiest thing to do is write a check. That is easier than praying. It is much more convenient than going, but we cannot escape the fact that the Great Commission has the word *go* in it. To be obedient to this command demands that some of us need to leave where we are. That does not just apply to nationals overseas. Every church is to send. *Go* applies to both American churches as well as churches around the world.

2. When our churches stop sending our own people, missions will eventually grind to a halt. It is healthy for some of us to be sacrificing our lives and giving up close proximity with loved ones for the sake of missions. When we have skin in the game, we stay engaged. Writing a check can be mechanical. Sending my kids and grandkids engages my heart.

3. Nationals are not always cheaper. The idea that you can hire four for the price of one assumes that missions is aimed at developing countries. The reality is that there are many places where salaries are better than in the USA. It could cost more than

$125,000 a year to support a national in Europe. Suddenly, this idea of supporting nationals is not so attractive. Would we support nationals if it costs more than sending one of our own?

4. Nationals are not always more effective. For instance, would we say that all pastors in the USA are equally effective? American pastors may know the language and culture, but some do better than others. The same is true overseas. Just knowing the language doesn't mean automatic success. The reality is that the gospel has often spread because an outsider came into a new culture and setting. We are all the product of missions. Without cross-cultural workers, the spread of the gospel stops.

5. The assumption that you can hire a national is based on the idea that there is a national to hire. In other words, the gospel is already there. But what about the 6000 unreached peoples of the world? Someone is going to have to learn a new language and adjust to a new culture in order to complete the Great Commission. Are we suggesting that only non-Americans should do cross cultures?

6. The great news is that the church around the world is rising to this occasion and launching missionaries into places that may be more difficult for Americans to go. If we finance all of these missions efforts, we rob the national church of the joy and obedience that comes with sending and supporting their own. Will our giving stimulate or discourage local giving? Will we create an unhealthy dependency? If we fund all missions

around the world, will that enhance the maturity of those churches? A few years ago I listened with fascination to an African pastor talk about why they were more effective in missions than Americans because of their poverty. Missions is not limited to affluent churches.

There is no way around the fact that the Great Commission is going to cost us a lot, but Jesus didn't give us a pass on missions if it became too expensive.

REASON #9: PERFECTIONISM

Training leaders requires letting others do ministry with the realization that they will not do it as well as you could do it. To train preachers, you have to relinquish your pulpit occasionally, but that could be embarrassing. What if the protégé really does a bad job? What will the congregation think? What if you have visitors? Will people be bored?

This drives perfectionists crazy. Those who are perfectionists have challenges when it comes to releasing ministry to others. There is a fine line between doing things with excellence and perfectionism. We obviously highly value ministry and are committed to doing the best we can. We can do well, but we can't be perfect. No matter how good you are, you are not perfect.

Your rejoinder might be that Jesus said, *Be perfect, therefore, as your heavenly Father is perfect* (Matthew 5:48). It is clear from scripture that we cannot attain sinless perfection in this lifetime, so the word here for *perfect* can also mean genuine, complete, mature in your behavior. We are to advance in our Christ-likeness, but we can never be without sin. A poor sermon is not a sin. Undeveloped skills are not a sin issue; it is a matter of development and learning.

This drives proud people crazy. Let's go ahead and admit it. If we give our pulpit over to someone and he does a lousy job, we will be embarrassed. We don't want people thinking badly about us or our church. Pride is thinking more of ourselves than we should, so why not admit it from the beginning that your church services are not perfect. No one expects us to be perfect so why act like we are. The more attractive trait is "genuine." People want to see that we are real. We should not fear the disapproval of others and should not be driven by feelings of insecurity.

INVERSE THINKING

Dave Brown, missionary to Africa, often says: "Pastors use leaders to build the church, but missionaries use the church to build leaders." Not just missionaries should be operating that way, however; pastors should also be using their church to build leaders. The congregation needs to understand that they are guinea pigs. Part of their ministry is to sit through someone's first sermon. Some congregation let you preach your first message, and you are probably embarrassed to recall how bad it was. Now it is your turn to return the favor.

In my book *Senders* I wrote the following:

> Local churches are like paper cups. They are designed by God to contain ministry, but they are disposable. The universal church is permanent. Local churches are not. I am totally committed to the centrality of the local church. I've spent my entire ministry focused on establishing local churches, so I am not questioning the importance of churches. But the reality is that local churches are temporary—especially buildings. They may last six months or sixty years, but sooner or

later they will cease to exist.

Here is the big idea. The local church is not the end goal—disciples are. Local churches are not eternal—people are. A church is not an institution; it is a group of Christians. So in that sense, a local church is a paper cup. Local churches are meant to be a temporary container for ministry. God intended the Christian life to take place within the context of local churches. They simply provide the forum for growth and ministry.

If we think of a local church as a porcelain cup, we may tend to be corporate and too institutional. We would try to build an empire instead of building people. The Great Commission is to make disciples. While church planting is a focal point of much missions activity, making disciples is the ultimate goal.

There is a difference between the goals and job descriptions of missionaries and pastors— a big difference. This major variance is not related to getting on an airplane. Missionaries are not just pastors who move to another country. Here is one difference: the goal of the missionary is not to shepherd a flock but to establish flocks" (Seger, Senders, 2016).

The pastor should have a missionary mindset. It is understandable that you may not wish to surrender your Sunday morning pulpit to someone who has never preached before, but there are many opportunities to train potential preachers in other ways. You might consider coaching people in the context of a Sunday school, small group Bible studies, other church meetings, nursing homes, or rescue mission services. To make those opportunities productive, it means that the pastor needs to be there to listen and then take the time after the event to debrief and coach.

POSSESSIVENESS AND PATIENCE

There are two more roadblocks to training leaders in addition to perfectionism. One is possessiveness and the other is patience. We love ministering so much we don't want to let go, and it takes longer to train someone else than just do it yourself. A father can wash his car in half the time than it takes to train his two young boys to wash the car. It means the job is going to take longer for the boys to do it.

Few pastors would claim that the church is theirs. Theologically, we all admit that the church belongs to Christ since He is the head of the church. That is what we say, but could it be that we have held back ownership of a particular local church. That possessiveness will keep us from handing over ministry to others who may not do it as well. To our credit, we love ministry. We really like what we are doing. We don't really want to give up our opportunity to preach, teach and pastor, but the reality is that there is plenty of opportunity to go around. There is job security in the gospel ministry since there will always be a need. We'll never run out of lost and broken people to reach and heal.

It does take patience to train others to minister. We can prepare a message faster if we don't have someone looking over our shoulder asking questions.

We could make that hospital visit and be home if we didn't have to coordinate schedules with a protégé. It takes time to first teach, then train, then debrief with someone as they learn the how-to of serving. Let's admit it . . . we don't have the patience to watch a novice stumble his way through the learning process.

The solution is love. 1 Corinthians 13:4 puts it simply this way: *Love is patient.* The antidote to my lack of patience is love. The determination to put others first is at the very heart of love and the solution to impatience. Loving others will pull us away from our perfectionism.

REASON #10: SELF-FOCUSED

The church I attend in Atlanta is going through a master-planning exercise. We have engaged consultants to help us think through how to update and improve the buildings that house our church. Notice that we are not looking to expand our facilities. We are planning to max out at 500. That may seem counterintuitive. Shouldn't a church have aspirations to be larger than it is right now?

ALIVE MEANS CHANGE AND REPRODUCTION

Here is the context of that decision. Our church wants to be a SENDING church. The process is simple:

1. Reach people through evangelism.
2. Disciple new believers to grow in Christ.
3. Train Leaders.
4. Send people out to start churches (both here and abroad).
5. Repeat.

We view our church as a factory that produces Christian workers. It is the aspiration of the church to launch out as many people to build "the" kingdom instead of "our" kingdom. That is a totally different mindset from many churches. It requires a pastor who has an open hand to let go of key people to bless other ministries and start churches around the world instead of building our own local assembly. It takes a pastor with a view to expanding the Body of Christ, not our manifestation of that body. It takes a pastor with ego subdued that does not measure success by how many people are gathered under "his" roof.

Jesus was enjoying a quiet evening with friends in Bethany, about a mile away from Jerusalem. He had been there before, so these were old friends. Perhaps they were reminiscing as they casually enjoyed a lengthy dinner reclining around a low table. In the middle of that calm evening, Mary rocked their world. It could not have been any more dramatic than if someone had rolled a hand grenade into the room. She took a pound of spikenard ointment and anointed the feet of Christ.

Incredibly, it was worth an annual salary. The average worker would earn about 1 denarius a day, so 300 denarii was equivalent to what a person would earn in a year. Two thousand years later you can almost hear the gasp in that room as they realized she had just expended the equivalent of tens of thousands of dollars-worth of perfume. In one moment, it was gone. She couldn't gather it back into the alabaster box. It just dissipated into the air, and all that remained was the aroma, which also had a short lifespan.

John 12 describes four reactions to Mary and what she had done.

1. Though Judas said the money could be better spent on the poor, he really wanted those funds in his own pocket.

2. Jesus commended her for her actions.

3. Jews came that evening *not only on account of him but also to see Lazarus, whom he had raised from the dead* (John 12:9). They were equally or possibly more interested in seeing what Jesus could do than seeing Jesus.

4. The chief priests were empire builders. *So the chief priests made plans to put Lazarus to death as well, because on account of him many of the Jews were going away and believing in Jesus* (John 12:10-11). They couldn't tolerate people following Jesus instead of themselves. Christ was eroding their influence and their empire. Their desire for followers was intense enough to drive them to murder anyone who would get in their way.

The chief priests were the religious leaders of the day. Could you imagine a pastor being so self-focused that he would hire a hit man to take out someone in the way of building his empire? While murder is too radical for a shepherd, it is possible that a pastor might want to eradicate the competition. Sending their best people from their church is certainly competition and obviously diminishes his empire.

A self-focused church will never be a sending church. It is not possible to be generous and self-focused at the same time. It doesn't make sense to send away the best and brightest leaders if you are looking to build a church. Yet that is exactly what the church at Antioch did in Acts 13.

Imagine what it would have been like that first Sunday after Paul and Barnabas left for the mission field. It is counterintuitive to send out your chief theologian and expositor. The offerings would be lower because of

Barnabas' absence. The counselling ministry was diminished without the chief encourager on the pastoral staff. It was a huge sacrifice to let go of those key leaders.

Some churches may be in survival mode, so it doesn't make sense to let go of key leaders. If a pastor has trained leaders, it would be nice to keep them around and benefit from his specific ministry.

Here is the big idea. The local church is not the end goal. Making disciples is the ultimate target. Local churches are not eternal—people are. A church is not an institution; it is a group of Christians. While we know all this, church leaders still operate like it is corporate and institutional. Success is not measured by the number of seats in the sanctuary, it is measured by whether we are helping people to grow in Christ and whether they are *observing whatsoever I have commanded you* (Matthew 28:19-20).

CONCLUSION

ONCE UPON A TIME . . .
By A. Timothy Heijermans, WEF Ministries

Once upon a time, some prophets and teachers were ministering in the First Christian Church at Antioch: Barnabas, Simeon called Niger, Lucius of Cyrene, Manaen (who had been brought up with Herod the tetrarch) and Saul. While they were worshipping the Lord and fasting, the Holy Spirit said, "Set apart for me Barnabas and Saul for the work to which I have called them."

So, the prophets and teachers sat down to discuss the Holy Spirit's proposal. They agreed from the outset that to send away some of the most gifted men of their group would be the height of folly. After all, they had a top-notch multiple-staff ministry going. What a shame to break things up prematurely!

Barnabas, for example, was urgently needed in Antioch. If he left town, would he ever finish his new book on "How to Nouthetically Exhort Gentile Converts"? What about the church counseling center he had been organizing since last year? And then, of course, his financial situation was certainly no detriment to the work; it would be suicidal to dispatch such a generous hearted member of the pastoral staff on some vaguely defined mission where beggars would prey on his good nature and thieves deftly pick his pockets.

And what about Saul? Why, it was unthinkable to send a bold pulpiteer into the bush. He was beginning to really shine there at Antioch. True enough, his exposition of the Old Testament was heavy at times, but with a few hints on sermon illustrations, body language and intonation, he would soon become far and away the most popular Bible teacher north of Jerusalem. Everyone knew it was unheard of to send experienced theologians into "pioneer" situations; why waste so much straight-from-the-shoulder power and expertise?

No! This idea of getting rid of Barnabas and Saul was no good. It violated all the time-honored principles of success in pastoral ministry. The best people move up the ladder, building big churches, acquiring prestige; they don't bother to start from scratch somewhere in Boondoggle Borough. And so, the decision of the church board was unanimous: The Reverends Barnabas and Saul MUST stay on at Antioch, and, to demonstrate their moral support, the church body later took official action to the effect that:

1. both pastors would receive a 10% pay increase each year for the next five years;

2. the church would pay all expenses for Saul's upcoming eye surgery;

3. traveling expense allowances for Barnabas and Saul would be doubled to handle the stiff, new Roman road taxes. And someone would be sent over to Barnabas' stable in two days to outfit his mule with a new bridle and harness;

4. Saul had done a great job with Gamaliel, but he needed an additional theological degree (it always enhances a church's reputation to have a couple of title-studded names on the staff). So why not give him a six-month sabbatical, all expenses paid? There were some outstanding post-doc courses right then at Jerusalem Evangelical Seminary; the church secretary would get Saul's application in the mail by week's end.

But what about the Holy Spirit's recommendation? **Someone** had to be sent to do this job, or the church would be found in direct conflict with the will of God. How about some of the church young people? Barnabas suggested his nephew, John Mark. He was certainly qualified in every way to move into new territory for God; he knew Simon Peter well, came from a good Christian home (he had a clear testimony and his mom was the leading lady in Jerusalem, right?). What more could be expected? As far as practical work in the ministry – well, experience was universally recognized as the best teacher. Little John would learn fast!

So, it was determined that John Mark and any other serious-minded Christian friends who wanted to see the word and serve the Lord would be commissioned forthwith. In three weeks, John Mark and two buddies packed their bags. The Board of Elders placed their hands on them and sent them off.

Unfortunately, things did not turn out as well as they might have. John Mark's mission folded in two months; contact with occult powers and raw heathendom were a bit too much. The group at Antioch grew considerably for some years. But Saul and Barnabas eventually had a falling out. There was a church split. Paul, as he came to be called by his Antiochan partisans, never did get around to using his fine seminary training in cross-cultural church growth. Nor did he ever have occasion to throw himself heart and soul into canonical correspondence. And so, the Bible was never completed; the Germanic hordes were never converted to Christianity; there never was a Reformation; North America was never populated by pietists and anabaptists fleeing oppression; there never was a fundamental-liberal debate.

Too bad. If only the First Christian Church at Antioch had not been so possessive, things could have been so different (Heijermans, 1982).

Works Cited

Greear, J. D. (2015). *Gaining by Losing: Why the Future Belongs to Churches That Send.* Grand Rapids: Zondervan. Retrieved from https://a.co/28EYUdQ

Greear, J. D. (n.d.). *Gaining By Losing: Why the Future Belongs to Churches That Send.* Retrieved June 24, 2020, from https://a.co/iBM5HxL

Heijermans, A. T. (1982, September/October). *Voice.*

Leeman, J. (2017). *World-Centered Church: How Scripture Brings Life and Growth to God's People.* Chicago: Moody Press.

Louw, J. P., & Nida, E. A. (1966). *Greek-English Lexicon of the New Testament: Based on Semantic Domains.* New York: United Bible Societies.

MacArthur, J. (1985). *I Corinthians.* Chicago: Moody Press.

Murrow, D. (2011). *Why Men Hate Going to Church.* Nashville: Nelson.

Seger, P. (2013). *Chief.* Monee: Sawubona Press.

Seger, P. (2016). *Senders.* Monee: Sawubona Press.

The Right Way to Manage Expats. (1999, March-April). Retrieved June 24, 2020, from Harvard Business Review: https://hbr.org/1999/03/the-right-way-to-manage-expats